Madaline & Kevin

To our children
Ari, Lylah, & Scarlett
Jack & Leo

May you always know how
deeply loved, wildly enjoyed and
endlessly pursued you are.

Inspired and Derived from the song "Adventures In Sleepland"
Written By:
Madaline Garcia-Heriges & Karin Simmons
Music Produced by Michael Farren
Text Copyright © 2021 WieRok Entertainment, LLC
Illustrations by Kalicia Moore, Copyright © 2021 WieRok Entertainment, LLC
Audio Copyright © 2021 WieRok Entertainment, LLC
This is a work of fiction. Names, characters, business, events and incidents are the products of the author's life experiences. Any resemblance to actual persons, living or dead, or actual events is intentional
All rights reserved. No part of this book may be reproduced in any form without written permission from the Publisher except for brief passages for use in reviews.

First Edition, English: July 2021

ISBN 978-1-7373309-0-5

Publisher:
WieRok Entertainment, LLC
188 Front St, #118-163, Franklin TN 37064
www.wierok.com

Direct Inquiries to: Publishing@WieRok.com

Direct Performing Artist/Music Inquiries to
TeamMaddie@MadalineGarcia.com

Find retail outlets at https://sleepland.MadalineGarcia.com Author website MadalineGarcia.com

Printed in China.

Adventures in Sleepland

Written by
**Madaline Garcia-Heriges
& Karin Simmons**

Illustrations by
Kalicia Moore

Up a high mountain all covered with snow,

With tea parties, hide and seek, dancing ballet.

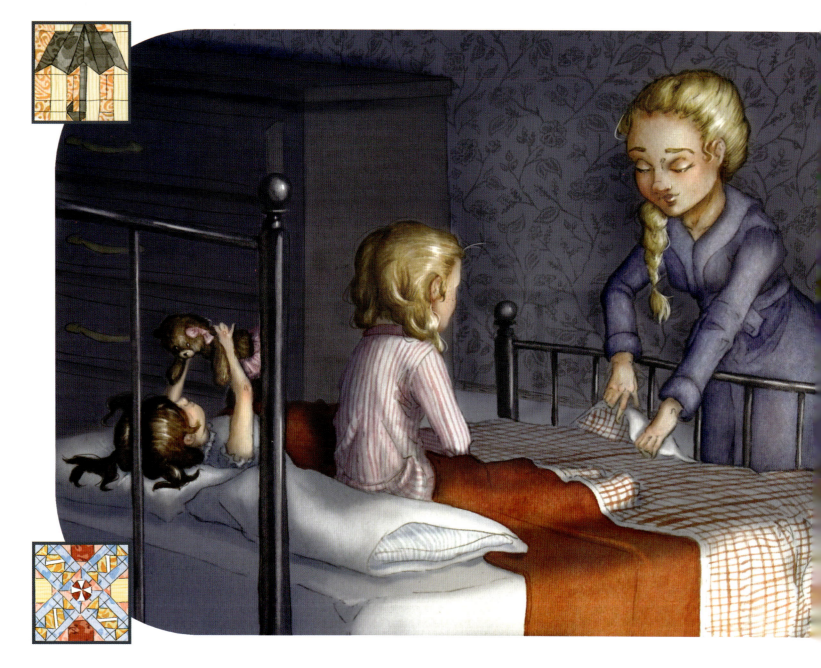

Adventures in Sleepland, what shall we see?

And gingerbread houses on peppermint lane.

Oh what a journey
   you'll take tonight!
I'll be here waiting
   come morning light.
For now my explorer,
   just close your eyes

And go on adventures in Sleepland.